IS GOD THERE?

Discovering who God is
Norman Warren

Is God there?

I think there's some great being
way up in space.

I believe there is someone – or something –
behind it all.

If there is a God, he's lost control.

I only believe what I can see,
and I can't see God.

You can't prove there's a God, can you!

Look at the mess the world is in. If there
was a God he would do something about it.

If there is a God of love, as people say,
why is there so much suffering and
violence and injustice?

I would like to think there is
someone I can turn to in trouble.

God? Can't possibly be interested in me!
There are so many millions of people.

I would love to believe there's a
God who is in charge.

Most people today believe in something or someone greater than themselves. Many would like to believe in God, but find it hard. God seems to be remote and unconcerned with our daily life and problems.

So is there a God?
Who is God?
What is God like?
Can I know God?

Is there a God?

God is the name given to the great and wonderful Creator. The one who made our world and our universe. The one who, alone, gives life. Either we believe in a Creator God, or we have to believe that everything happens by chance.

In 'The Sound of Music', Maria sings: 'Nothing comes from nothing, nothing ever could . . . .' This is true both emotionally and scientifically. Of course we cannot prove that there is a God by reason or by logical argument. You cannot put God into a test-tube and analyse him. You cannot prove love in this way either. That does not mean love does not exist! Scientific proof is good up to a point, but it is limited.

Philosophers who deny the existence of God find they have to put God back into their thinking by using another word or expression — 'The Absolute', 'The Life Force' or 'The Ground of Existence'. They have to do this because the amazing universe and the world in which we live demand a master designer, architect, engineer and artist. We call this great being God. As we look at this more closely, it is quite reasonable to conclude that the universe and our world were thought out and brought into being by a person far greater than us in power and intelligence. Johann Kepler, the founder of physical astronomy, said of his studies and discoveries: 'O God, I am thinking your thoughts after you.'

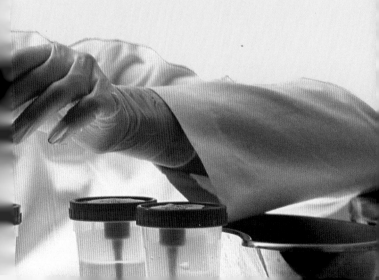

Who made God?

God is the name given to this great being behind
our world and our universe. Where did God
come from? Who made God?

We live in time, so we have a beginning and an
end. We are all born and we will all die. Just
because we are like this, we think that God must
be like this too. But he is not. He is very different.

The Bible tells us (and it is obvious if you think
about it) that God has no beginning and no end.
He is not limited by time — hours, days, weeks
and years — as we are.

If someone made God, then that
someone would have to be
greater than God. Think
for a moment of
space. It has no
beginning and

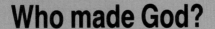

no end. It stretches on and on and on! This is something our limited minds find very hard to take in. We are conditioned all the time by our own lifespan, and by what we can see and know and understand – and we think that is the end of it. God is far greater than our little minds can take in, just as the vastness of space – stars millions of light-years away – is beyond our understanding.

Who made God? No-one! He is the source of all life, behind all creation. He is not limited by time, as we are. He has always been there. He is there now, and he will always be there. He never changes, as we do. He never grows old or weak. He has no beginning and no end. God is the one unchanging factor in an ever-changing world. He is the same yesterday, today and forever!

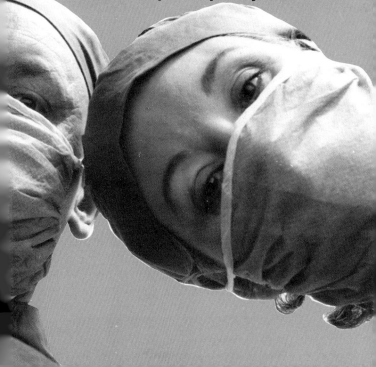

God the Creator

We live in a world of outstanding beauty and order.
The vastness and mystery of our universe all point to
a creator of imagination and of amazing power and
skill. Running through the whole world of nature
are clear signs of careful design and natural
laws. The movements of the stars and planets
are so ordered and precise that Greenwich
mean time is worked out from them.

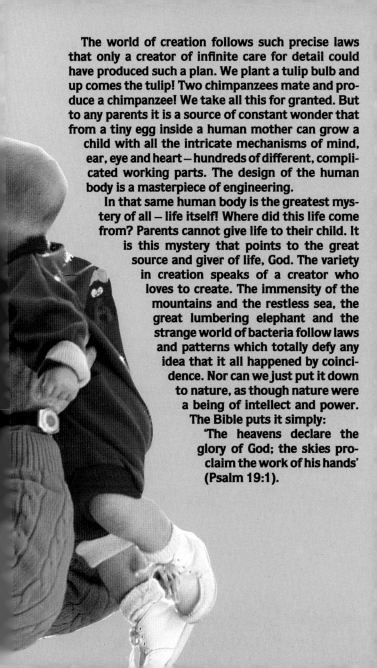

The world of creation follows such precise laws
that only a creator of infinite care for detail could
have produced such a plan. We plant a tulip bulb and
up comes the tulip! Two chimpanzees mate and pro-
duce a chimpanzee! We take all this for granted. But
to any parents it is a source of constant wonder that
from a tiny egg inside a human mother can grow a
child with all the intricate mechanisms of mind,
ear, eye and heart — hundreds of different, compli-
cated working parts. The design of the human
body is a masterpiece of engineering.

In that same human body is the greatest mystery of all — life itself! Where did this life come
from? Parents cannot give life to their child. It
is this mystery that points to the great
source and giver of life, God. The variety
in creation speaks of a creator who
loves to create. The immensity of the
mountains and the restless sea, the
great lumbering elephant and the
strange world of bacteria follow laws
and patterns which totally defy any
idea that it all happened by coinci-
dence. Nor can we just put it down
to nature, as though nature were
a being of intellect and power.
The Bible puts it simply:

'The heavens declare the
glory of God; the skies pro-
claim the work of his hands'
(Psalm 19:1).

How did it all begin?

Geologists tell us that our Earth is millions of years old. They can work out the age of the rocks fairly accurately. Was our Earth once part of another planet? If so, which one? Was there a gigantic explosion? We simply do not know. Then we turn to the Bible, and we are told that the world was made in six days. How can this be?

We have to remember that scientific work on the origins of our Earth is still theory. We also need to remember that the Bible is not a book of science, written in modern scientific language. The early books of the Bible were written over 3,000 years ago.

In the simple description of creation in the book of Genesis, the Hebrew word for day can mean not only 24 hours but also an age, or period of time. When we understand this, we see the story of creation unfolding in a new way — in six *stages* of creation. The Bible does not

discuss mechanics, but it does speak clearly of the creative activity of God. And the climax is the creation of man. 'Adam' is simply the Hebrew word for man — the first man.

We do not know whether the first true man, '*homo sapiens*', came from other animal life. But the difference in intelligence between man and other animals is vast, and increasing numbers of natural scientists seem to be following the Bible account of a special creation. This shows that man is in some way made in the image of his Creator God: able to think, choose and love; with a mind, a soul and free will, and so able to make rational decisions.

The course of history shows how man has used the great, creative gifts given to him, though sadly, not always for the benefit of himself and his fellows.

There are few greater evidences for the existence of a Creator God than the world of living creatures, at the head of which is the human race, endowed with remarkable and varied skills and abilities.

The invisible God

'I only believe what I can see! There can't be a God because I can't see God.'

You can't see your brains – but that doesn't mean they aren't there!

There are, of course, many things in everyday life that we cannot see – and yet we know they are there. We cannot see the wind. But we know it is there, because we can see its effects as it ruffles the water on a lake or blows through the trees.

Electricity is something else we can't see. But we know it's there when we switch on the light. We can see what electricity does, even though we can't actually see it. We can certainly feel it if we are unfortunate enough to get an electric shock! Its power can be tremendous, driving a long train at high speeds – but we can't see it.

We can't see the air. But we know it's there because we can't live without air.

We can't see love. But we know it's there in those who care for us.

We can't see God. But we know God is there because of the wonderful world all around us — a world full of beauty, colour and skilful design.

Things don't happen by chance. In the writing of a book, the words don't fly through the air and by chance land in the right order. Someone has to put the book together. Every book needs an author, every piece of music a composer, every painting an artist, every building an architect. Things like this don't happen by chance. Nor could the world have happened by chance. Someone had to plan it, design it and create it. This great designer, architect and creator we call God.

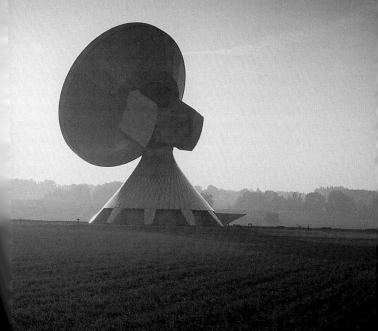

We can't see God with our eyes, but we can see his handiwork everywhere we look. God doesn't have a human body like us. He is infinite, beyond time, and not subject to time as we are. This does not mean that God does not have personality. God can love, think, plan, design and create. God has all the traits of personality, but no weak points, no flaws, no mistakes.

Jesus said, 'God is spirit' – full of active energy, life and purpose, with no limits in time or space. God cannot be confined to things or places.

Our spirit, or personality – what we are deep down – is the part of us which lasts when our physical bodies have disintegrated. Our spirit is the part of us that dreams dreams. It is the source of all our ideals, thoughts and desires. God is all this and more ... to perfection! No wonder Jesus continued that we must worship this God 'in spirit and in truth' (John 4:24).

God is beauty

In our world we are surrounded with beauty and colour. Tiny insects, tropical fish, the variety of colours in bird-life, flowers and hedgerows all radiate a beauty that even the greatest artist can never begin to match.

Who has not been filled with wonder at the sight of a sunset, with the ever-changing colours of crimson, orange and gold mingling with the blue of the sky or the dark green of the hills? Is this all sheer chance?

Our world and all creation could have been a uniform grey or brown. No doubt life could have gone on just the same, featureless and colourless – all things necessary for life could still have been there.

Not only are we surrounded by colour and beauty – we have also been given an appreciation of sounds and music and a sense of smell. So we can enjoy all God's creation to the full – the scent of the rose, the song of the nightingale, the design of the snowflake. Jesus said, 'See how the lilies of the field grow... Yet I tell you that not even Solomon in all his splendour was dressed like one of these...' (Matthew 6:29).

All this beauty and artistry could never have happened by chance. They tell us something about the Artist Creator. God loves colour and beauty. He has given us an overwhelmingly lavish amount of it everywhere we look, if only we have eyes to see!

God is just

Our world obeys certain laws — laws of gravity, laws of creation and procreation — all working to a careful plan. Law and justice is important to us and to our life in the community.

We have a sense of right and wrong. We feel deeply that justice is important and should be seen to be done. If an old lady is beaten up by thugs, we want justice to be done and the crime to be punished. We feel rightly aggrieved if someone jumps the queue. If we feel this, how much more does God, who has made us like this. He is a God of law and order — perfect justice. He can never make a mistake, because he knows all the facts as well as people's thoughts and motives. We can hide nothing from him.

However much we desire justice, the judge and jury are still fallible and human, and cannot know all the facts or all the thoughts of those involved in a trial. God is not limited like that. He is just, and demands truth and justice. He misses nothing! God cannot overlook wickedness and dishonesty, and his judgement slowly but surely works out, in this life and certainly in the next.

It may seem that some people get away with things in this life. They may do so for a time — even for years — but they cannot finally escape God's judgement. War criminals may still be in hiding, and so escape human sentence. But God knows exactly what has been done and no one can escape his judgement. The Bible puts it bluntly: 'We will all stand before God's judgement seat' (Romans 14:10).

So does God punish us through natural disasters — floods, hurricanes and earthquakes?

Natural disasters are part of our world; we have to live with them. There are always natural scientific explanations as to why they happen. It is unlikely that God always sends them; we simply do not know. But certainly he allows such things as part of the creative order. They remind us how frail we are, and how much we need God.

Doubtless certain disasters can be seen as a judgement on wickedness; the story of Sodom and Gomorrah in the Bible provides one example. But for the most part, natural disasters have fairly clear, natural reasons. Some areas of the world are more prone to certain disasters than others. This is a fact of life, and God cannot be blamed if people live in such areas. It is part of the risk we all take in living on this earth.

God is everywhere

Because we are human we can only be in one place at a time. God is not limited by space or time. This is the beautiful way the Psalmist in the Bible describes this:

'Lord, you have examined me and you know me.
You know everything I do;
from far away you understand my thoughts.
You see me, whether I am working or resting;
you know all my actions.
Even before I speak,
you already know what I will say.
You are all round me on every side;
you protect me with your power.
Your knowledge of me is too deep;
it is beyond my understanding.
Where could I go to escape from you?
Where could I get away from your presence?
If I went up to heaven, you would be there;
if I lay down in the world of the dead,
you would be there.
If I flew away beyond the east
or lived in the farthest place in the west,
you would be there to lead me,
you would be there to help me'
(Psalm 139:1–10).

No matter where you are or where you look, there is the presence of the Creator God. In every form of life — human, animal, insect or plant, God is at work, for he is the source of life. We cannot create life; we can only use what is already there. Wherever there is beauty in creation, or beauty created by human skill, God has been at work, for he is the giver of all beauty and all human talent.

Whether or not a composer or artist believes in God, he has given them the eye, the ear and the mind to create beauty. It is sad that so many great artists have lived such immoral lives. Yet they used and developed the gifts God had given them, whether or not they ever acknowledged this fact. We can enjoy the beauty of their God-given gifts.

God has given us free will to make choices and decisions, ideally for the good of all. Sadly, we see this precious gift misused for selfish ends. But even here we can detect God's purpose slowly being worked out. A study of history will show the will of God overruling the pride and evil of man in the fall of nations and of dictators. He is the God of the past, present and future. History is his story, following his plan, however hard we find it to detect it.

God is love

Page after page in the Bible shows us that God is love. On countless occasions he has made himself known to men and women as a loving father who cares deeply for his children. His nature is love, and he is the source of love. Whenever there is any act of kindness or compassion, God is behind it. It is he who has given to human beings the precious gifts of being able to give and receive love. No matter that people do not believe in God or acknowledge him; all love comes from him. No God, no love!

It was God's love of making things that brought about the universe and the world of creation. It is his love that holds it together.

In one of the most moving descriptions of God's love we hear God say:

> 'I took my people up in my arms,
> but they did not acknowledge that I took care of them.
> I drew them to me with affection and love.
> I picked them up and held them to my cheek;
> I bent down to them and fed them' (Hosea 11:3–4).

King David described God as a shepherd. Psalm 23 has been a source of inspiration and faith for generations of people. In it we see that God's love gives rest and peace, strength in times of trouble, and guidance in danger. He stays close to his children when they are fearful and worried. Finally he brings them safe to his heavenly home when their earthly life ends, to be with him for ever.

Nowhere do we see the love of God more clearly than in the life and teaching of Jesus. It was love that brought him to our world in the first place. It was love that took him to the cross to die for us. It was love that raised him to life on the first Easter day. Love came down at Christmas and it came to stay.

How can I know God?

'Can a man, by searching, find God?'

'Oh that I knew where I might find him.'
Modern sentiments? No, they were expressed
over 3,000 years ago. We have seen something
of the grandeur and greatness of the Creator
God. He is far beyond our human understanding.
His thoughts are so much higher than ours. We
are not clever enough to find him ourselves. He
lives beyond time and space, and he is not subject to them as we are. He is infinite in power
and wisdom. We are frail in comparison. We
cannot find him on our own. But we can see his
work in creation, in history, and in our own
amazing human bodies.

Every tribe and race of man since the dawn of creation has tried to find God, to worship some being greater than themselves. This has often shown itself in very strange, even horrific ways, in sacrifices. There is something deep down in human beings that is searching for that Infinite Being, for God. All the great religions of the world are part of that search.

If we are to find out more about God, he has to reveal himself in a clearer way to us. He has shown himself in his creation, but this is only a hazy revelation. He has shown himself in making his will known to holy men and women who

have longed to know him and obey him. He has shown himself through mighty acts in history.

All these reveal something of God. But the final moment of revelation came in Jesus. As we look at Jesus we see God in person. Philip, one of his followers, said to Jesus: 'Show us the Father; that is all we need.' Jesus answered:

'Whoever has seen me has seen the Father' (John 14:8, 9).

John, in his Gospel, is careful to show that Jesus did not come into existence at Bethlehem. Jesus has always existed, and his birth at Bethlehem was simply the way he chose to enter our world. So John, who knew Jesus well described him:

'He was with God, and he was the same as God. From the very beginning the Word was with God. Through him God made all things.. (He) was the source of life. (He) became a human being and, full of grace and truth, lived among us. We saw his glory, the glory which he received as the Father's only Son' (John 1).

One Way

Jesus is the one way to God. He was not only fully human, he was also fully divine. He was God and man perfectly joined together, perfect in life, in truth and in love.

The closer we look at Jesus, the more we marvel. His wonderful teaching, which no other earthly teacher has ever begun to match, was backed up by an equally wonderful life. He was at home with all people, accepting all people, ready to help and heal. He opened up to us Heaven itself as he spoke of the Kingdom of God right here among us.

So great was Jesus' love that he was willing to die for us. In an amazing way he took on himself all the weight of human sin and guilt. Peter, who watched all this, described it in this way:

'For Christ died for sins once and for all, a good man on behalf of sinners in order to lead you to God.'

'Christ himself carried our sins in his body to the cross' (1 Peter 3:18; 2:24).

He rose again from the grave and is alive. He longs to make himself known to us all, to forgive us and cleanse us, to give us his Spirit and bring us to eternal life.

Towards the end of his life, the apostle John was given a lovely picture, which he has shared with us. The risen Lord is speaking: 'Listen! I stand at the door and knock; if anyone hears my voice and opens the door, I will come into his house and eat with him and he will eat with me' (Revelation 3:20).

Your life is like a house. Jesus waits outside. He will not force his way in, for that is never love's way. He wants to be invited in, but the handle is on the inside. Only you can open the door. You can come to know God in a real and personal way by opening the door to Jesus Christ and inviting him to come in and live in your heart and life.

The open door to God

If you want to open your life to Jesus and invite him in, you might find this prayer helpful. Pray it phrase by phrase, quietly and thoughtfully, thinking carefully about what you are saying and doing.